JESUS CRUCIFIED FOR ME

JESUS CRUCIFIED FOR ME

PAUL TUCKER

THE EVANGELICAL PRESS

PROVIDENCE HOUSE, 3 SPEKE ROAD, LONDON, S.W.11

First published 1966

PRINTED AT THE BURLINGTON PRESS, FOXTON, NEAR CAMBRIDGE, ENGLAND

TO MY FATHER AND MOTHER

FOREWORD

These sermons are published in a form very similar to that in which they were preached to a group of East London people. They are designedly straightforward. In these days when it is fashionable for preachers and others who speak for Christianity to be highly intellectual and controversial in their utterances, I make no apology for a restatement in the simplest language of what is revealed to us in the gospels concerning the crucifixion of Jesus Christ. If they help to make the meaning of the cross of Christ more real and personal to any as yet unfamiliar with the Christian gospel, I shall be more than satisfied. "God was in Christ, reconciling the world unto himself"—His death and its meaning is as relevant in this twentieth century as it was when it actually took place.

PAUL TUCKER.

East London Tabernacle,
London, E.3.
February, 1966.

CONTENTS

I sometimes think about His cross,
And shut my eyes, and try to see
The cruel nails, and crown of thorns,
And Jesus crucified for me.

William Walsham How.

INTRODUCTION

". . . And when they had come to the place which is called Calvary there they crucified him."

Luke 23: 33.

Jesus did not die alone, "He was numbered with the transgressors" (Isa. 53 : 12).

There were three crosses upon the hill of Calvary, two of them occupied by thieves, and the central cross by the best Man who ever lived upon this earth. The best man? More than that, for He was God in the form and flesh of man.

Thirty-three years before this event Jesus had been born in a stable at Bethlehem in Judea. After a brief stay in Egypt His mother and her husband, Joseph, returned with Him as a young child and settled in Nazareth, where He grew up as the son of Mary, and of Joseph the village carpenter. At about thirty years of age He went to Jordan to be baptized by His cousin John "the Baptist". This marked the beginning of His public work.

He went about doing good, teaching, healing, saving; with Him were twelve men whom He called from various walks of life to be His disciples. The common people heard Him gladly; but the rulers became increasingly envious of His popularity until their jealousy drove them into a conspiracy to bring about His death.

He was arrested, then tried—a mockery of justice; He was spat upon, His beard was plucked, a crown of thorns was forced upon His head and a multitude of misguided people were roused by a few fanatics into clamouring for His death. The horrifying moment came when the streets of Jerusalem rang with the cry, "Crucify Him! crucify Him!"

He was led away to the hill of Calvary, on the way stumbling under the crushing burden of the cross that He was forced to carry. When they reached the fateful spot He was nailed to His cross, which was lifted and then dropped into its socket in the ground. Every bone in His sensitive body was jolted, His nerves shivered with the excruciating pain.

There upon the cross Jesus spoke His last words before He yielded up His life . . . .

I. FATHER . . . FORGIVE

"Father, forgive them for they know not what they do."   Luke 23:34.

The Lord Jesus Christ prayed thus from the cross. He was suffering agony untold, and dying a shameful death. Artists depicting the scene sometimes show Him wearing a loin-cloth, but all who hung upon a Roman cross hung there stark naked, and our Saviour was no exception.

> *"Bearing shame and scoffing rude,*
> *In my place condemned He stood."*

In such a situation the Lord Jesus prayed, yet not for Himself but for others. It would have been understandable had He prayed for Himself. For it is not wrong to pray for oneself when in difficulty or peril. Peter prayed when he began to sink in the boisterous waves of Galilee, "Lord, save me". But the Lord who answered Peter's cry was now Himself overwhelmed, yet He prayed not for Himself, but for others, who were not His friends, but His enemies. He pleaded for the very people responsible for His death, "Father, forgive *them*".

Authorities tell us that the Greek can be translated "Jesus kept on praying". It would appear that He did not pray one isolated prayer, but that He prayed continually. As they drove the nails into His flesh He prayed, "Father, forgive . . .". As they callously raised the cross and then dropped it into its socket in the ground; as they passed by jeering, "He saved others, himself he cannot save"; as the soldiers

11

unconcernedly gambled for His clothes, we can hear Him uttering this prayer. We cannot be sure how often the Lord Jesus stormed the throne of grace on behalf of His persecutors; but of this we can be sure, that it is one who prays in this way for others that we need as our Saviour and intercessor.

Our Lord was a praying Man

This was not an isolated illustration of our Lord's praying. In every recorded facet of His life prayer was predominant. His public life began with prayer; Luke tells us that as He was baptised in Jordan He was praying. Repeatedly, in the three years which followed, the writers of the gospels tell us that Jesus prayed.

Now, at the close of His earthly ministry, the Lord Jesus Christ was engaged in prayer. Three times He prayed on the cross, at the beginning and end of His suffering, and in the midst of it. So from first to last our Lord's passion was bathed in holy conversation and communion with God. His earthly ministry was now over. He could no longer use His hands to multiply the loaves and fishes, or to touch and heal the lepers, for His hands were impaled on the cross. He could no longer use His feet to go to the needy with love and with help, for His feet were nailed to the wood. He could not call little children to His side, for He hung above their reach, and soon His side would be pierced by a spear. He could neither move, nor touch, nor help. What could He do? He could do something very wonderful, He could pray.

There are servants of the Lord Jesus Christ whose active life is drawing to its close, they can no longer serve Him as they once did. There are some who are prisoners in their own rooms or inactive on a hospital bed. They can no longer go and tell for their Master, or worship with His people at God's house. But like their Lord they can pray. Who knows but that their praying accomplishes more in the kingdom of God than much of the activity of others?

We cannot measure the power or the value of our Saviour's prayers upon the cross. He addressed His "Father", showing that He had not lost His consciousness of His unique relationship to God. It is the more significant if we remember how unjustly our Lord had been treated—falsely accused, mocked and forsaken. We can but marvel at His faith. When righteousness is trampled under foot and wrong stalks and triumphs in the world, when goodness and purity are on the scaffold and evil on the throne some might lose confidence in the love and power of God. But the faith of Jesus Christ did not waver, it shone brightest in the darkest hour, and His trust in His Father was as strong as ever— "*Then* said Jesus, Father . . .".

When man was doing his worst, we see the love of Jesus at its best. "When they had come to the place which is called Calvary, there they crucified him . . . then said Jesus, Father forgive them . . .". In this particular situation He pleaded that they might be forgiven. The murderers, the bigoted religious leaders who hated Him, the howling mob lusting for His blood, the soldiers completing their awful task, around them all He threw the mantle of His prayer, "Forgive them".

The Lord Jesus Christ could pray this because He had forgiveness in His own heart towards them. Early in His ministry on another hill He sat with His disciples to teach them the ways of His kingdom in what we know as "the sermon on the mount". One thing He said to them was, "You have heard that it hath been said, an eye for an eye, and a tooth for a tooth: . . . But I say unto you, Love your enemies . . . and pray for them . . ." (Matt. 5 : 38, 44). Now on the grim hill of Calvary Jesus was putting into practise His own teaching. He was loving and praying for

His enemies. What He prayed for was that their greatest need might be met—the forgiveness of their sins. This is surely the greatest need of anyone at any time.

We all had a part in the death of the Lord Jesus

We look at this scene and perhaps could wish to detach ourselves from it. We may think that these people were worse than we are. Yet if we are honest we must acknowledge that there are sins in our hearts which parallel the sins that brought Jesus Christ to the cross. Judas Iscariot betrayed the Lord Jesus and made possible His arrest. Why did he do it? Because he was greedy where money was concerned. He was the bursar for the disciples, he carried the bag, and was not above helping himself to the contents (John 12 : 6). For thirty pieces of silver he betrayed the Son of God. Is there not a little Judas in us all? Have we never coveted that little bit more money?

The chief priests were willing to pay the thirty silver pieces for information about the Lord Jesus Christ which would enable them to be rid of Him. They were jealous of Him, for Pilate knew that for envy they had betrayed Him (Matt. 27 : 18). Is jealousy an emotion of which we are ignorant?

Pilate knew that the Lord was innocent, yet he delivered Him to the soldiers to be crucified. His own position and prestige were at stake and meant more to him than justice. Is the world free of men who put their own prestige and popularity above all other considerations? Wishing for that little bit more, envious when others are liked and admired more than we are, prepared to be less than scrupulously just and honourable in all our dealings with others in order to keep our name—these are emotions and traits common to humanity. They reached their logical conclusion in the death of Jesus Christ on the cross. They are our sins too, and forgiveness is our greatest need.

The Scribes and Pharisees murmured, "Who can forgive sins but God only" (Mark 2 : 7). Jesus answered them, "The Son of man (Himself) hath *power on earth* to forgive sins". He said to the man who was paralysed, "Thy sins be forgiven thee" (Matt. 9 : 2). To the woman who had been a sinner He said, "Neither do I condemn thee, go and sin no more" (John 8 : 11). Yet now He *prays the Father* to forgive. Is it fanciful to suggest that the Lord Jesus was no longer on "earth" as the Son of Man? He was suspended between heaven and earth and was now beginning His ministry of intercession, which He continued after His ascension to His Father in Heaven. What, under the old agreement with God, necessitated the priest, the altar and the sacrifice to accomplish, Jesus Christ, the Lamb of God, was fulfilling in Himself, as He laid down His life as an atonement for the sins of the world. On the basis of the sacrifice of Himself, He could ask that the people be forgiven. In fact he began then, what He continues still to do—to make intercession for us at the throne of grace.

"They know not what they do"

There is in sin a strange combination of ignorance and knowledge. Though Jesus in compassion said they know not what they do, He was by no means excusing them. The basis of their forgiveness was not their ignorance of their sinfulness. Pilate, in all probability, did not know that Jesus of Nazareth was the eternal Son of God, but he did know that the Man standing before him was no ordinary man and that He was innocent of the crime of which He was accused. The chief priests did not recognise in Jesus their Messiah, but they must have been conscious in some part of the envy and hatred in their hearts which drove them to their cruel and unjust decision.

When Jesus prayed, "They know not what they do", He was not excusing their behaviour or exaggerating their ignorance, but acknowledging the limitations of their knowledge. They were not aware of the enormity of their crime in crucifying the Son of God, the Lord of glory and, in spitting upon and jeering at the everlasting Son of the Father, the One whom angels and archangels and all the company of heaven worship and adore. This is a very solemn aspect of sin.

When we sin we may realise to a small degree our guilt, but we may be unaware of the magnitude and consequences of it. Sin is a little bit of hell let loose. We cannot evaluate the repercussions it may cause. This is tragically illustrated by many trends in society today of which only one example is the rise in the divorce rate. Marriage breakdowns are now common. What is the chain of events? A marriage is dissolved, the partners go their own way, the children remain with one or the other, but are denied the security of a happy home life. They in turn grow up with problems which they carry into their adult life. We see an increase in the disintegration of family life, until the situation in many cases is irreparable and the very basis of society is undermined. It begins with the selfishness of one or two people, but the enormity of their action is reflected in its far-reaching consequences and repercussions throughout the generations that follow.

How this prayer was answered

According to the Acts of the Apostles, it was answered in a very remarkable way. Our Lord had gathered around Him a company of Apostles, who were to preach and teach His gospel after His ascension. They were to preach in the power of the Holy Spirit and, when they did so, men and women would be convicted of their sin, and with conviction would come a realisation of the awfulness of their sin in having a part in the death of Jesus Christ.

At Pentecost Peter preached, charging more than three thousand people with the death of Christ, "You have taken Jesus and with wicked hands have crucified and slain Him. God has made Him Lord and Christ and the One you crucified is now exalted. He is living, and unless you repent you will answer to Him as your judge" (See Acts 2). At this they cried out, "Men and brethren what shall we do?" The truth so impressed itself upon their hearts that they repented of their sin and were baptised, identifying themselves with the Lord they had helped to crucify.

Not long after this a lame man was healed at the gate of the temple, and a great multitude of people crowded around Peter in Solomon's colonnade, and heard him explain the secret of the miracle. God, he said, had raised up the One whom they had crucified, and through His power this man had been healed. Again he charged them, "Ye denied the Holy One and the Just, and desired a murderer to be granted unto you; and killed the Prince of life, whom God raised from the dead" (Acts 3 : 14-15). But he added words of comfort, "Brethren, I know that through ignorance you did it . . ." echoing our Lord's words, ". . . they know not what they do". As a result of Peter's words five thousand men were added to the Lord. The prayer from the cross was assuredly answered.

Let us not assume, however, that the Lord Jesus Christ was asking God to cancel the sins of everyone, everywhere, irrespective of their attitude. According to the teaching of the Scriptures, forgiveness involves, even presupposes, repentance. It was not a blanket cancellation of the sins of all those involved in the crucifixion for which He prayed, rather He was saying something like this, "Father, do not interfere with these murderers, do not strike them down, postpone

Thy judgment upon them, until they have the opportunity to understand and repent of what is happening".

Forgive is a word which is translated *suffer* in the incident where our Lord rebuked the disciples for preventing the mothers from bringing their little ones to Him. "Suffer little children to come unto me, and forbid them not". In other words "Don't interfere with them, permit them to come to Me". So on the cross our Saviour prayed that God would not interrupt their maliciousness, that He would delay the hand of justice, knowing that in making intercession for the transgressors many would ultimately learn the deeper meaning of His death, and through it would be "ransomed, healed, restored, forgiven".

II. A PROMISE OF PARADISE

"Today shalt thou be with me in paradise."

Luke 23:43.

In imagination we come to the green hill outside the city wall of Jerusalem and see three crosses lifted against the sky. When the Lord Jesus Christ died, He did not die alone, for on either side of Him was a cross, and on each cross a thief. This was no chance happening, nor was it of mere human devising.

Doubtless those who brought Jesus Christ to the cross thought they were insulting Him, that this was the last great affront, that He should be crucified between two common criminals. It was as if in their gloating, they said, "While He was alive He mixed with outcasts and traitors, He ate with them and even served them, now let Him die with them". They, in their hatred, could not realise that there was a superior Power overruling all that was happening. Yet centuries earlier the evangelical prophet had said, "He was numbered with the transgressors; and he bare the sin of many and made intercession for the transgressors" (Isa. 53:12). Without hesitation we can say that from eternity God had planned the day and the details of our Saviour's death. That day saw Him crucified between two thieves, one on His right hand and the other on His left.

Salvation by grace

We may for ever be grateful that our Saviour suffered such humiliation, for His experience portrays for us one of the clearest pictures of salvation by grace that we can ever see.

19

What would some of the closest followers of the Lord Jesus not have given to have been the first to enter paradise with Him? Yet this privilege was granted to one of the most unworthy and unexpected persons imaginable—"The dying thief rejoiced to see . . ." what others were denied.

Our Lord was not long on the cross before He was in conversation with one of the malefactors. In all probability these men had served in Barabbas' gang and were violent and merciless men. As we look at the one who appealed to Jesus it is obvious that he was without moral background and had nothing to offer that would commend him to God's favour. His life was wasted and he was about to die, so he would have no opportunity to make amends on earth for his conduct.

Sometimes a man who serves a prison sentence learns from his bitter experience, and seeks, when he can, to make redress for his past misdeeds. He may walk the hard road of rehabilitation in society, and by so doing recover his dignity as a man. But this dying thief on the cross had no such opportunity. He had no future on earth in which he might become a disciple of Jesus Christ, and in His service make amends for his failures. No talents or riches or gifts were his to offer—he had nothing—yet he was accepted by God and received into the company of those who walk and talk with Jesus Christ. He was saved by grace alone, as Paul says, "Not by works of righteousness which we have done but according to his mercy he saved us".

The conversation between our Lord and the thief gives the lie to many false views concerning the way of salvation. It is taught by some that, to become a Christian, a person must be baptised, then attend the service of communion and be a loyal member of the church, and that in subscribing to its rites and ceremonies, he is made acceptable to God. It is quite clear that one who already is a Christian will do all of these things, but it is equally clear that not one of these, nor all of them together, can make a person a child of God. The dying thief could not be baptised. Water could not be sprinkled on his head, nor could he be immersed. He could not come to the Lord's table and partake of bread and wine. He certainly could not be made a member of a church on earth. Only a few more hours were his to live, and those he must spend straitened upon a cross. Yet he was saved, because salvation is not in any way a result of our observance of ordinances, but is a consequence of our acceptance and forgiveness by God through the Lord Jesus Christ.

There are some who teach that before it is possible to reach heaven we must go through the purifying fires of purgatory. If anyone needed to pass through purgatory it was the dying thief. Yet the Lord Jesus did not say to him, "Today shalt thou be with me in purgatory". It would not have been very comforting to a man who was even then going through the excruciating pains of crucifixion. Scripture teaches that we are justified by the merits of Jesus Christ, and cleansed from all sin by His blood. What His blood has effected cannot be improved upon by any purgatorial flames.

> *"What can wash away my stain?*
> *Nothing but the blood of Jesus.*
> *What can make me whole again?*
> *Nothing but the blood of Jesus."*

Immediate entry into paradise is a definite promise given to one particular man. Jesus says to one of the thieves, "Today thou shalt be with me in paradise". He did not say this to the other thief, or to the soldiers, or to the crowd around them. The other thief died still ridiculing the Lord. The one to whom the promise was made was the one who appealed to the Lord for His consideration. An old writer remarks, "One thief was saved, in order that no one need despair; one thief was lost in order that no one dare presume." Let none presume upon the mercy of God, nor think that he may live just as he pleases without reference or giving account to God; but neither let anyone despair, as he may well be tempted to do, for in the experience of the dying thief we see that there is hope for the worst amongst us.

This interview would not lead one to believe that the soul sleeps at death as it is taught by some. They say that death is followed by a state of unconsciousness, or of suspended animation in which we are completely unaware of ourselves, and we awake from this sleep only at the second coming of the Lord Jesus Christ. But this teaching is not supported by the words of Christ Himself. His words were not, "Today thou shalt fall asleep and remain unconscious until I return to earth again". His promise was, "Today you will be with me in paradise". Elsewhere in the New Testament we read of our Lord's activity between His death and His resurrection. So His assurance to the thief can mean nothing less than that he would actively and consciously be in fellowship with Him beyond the grave.

This teaching is borne out by other verses, such as the Psalmist's assurance of his reception by God after death (Psa. 73 : 24); and Paul's concept of fellowship with Jesus Christ being even better in the heavenly state (Phil. 1 : 23). The abysmal sadness of this scene on Calvary is thus transformed by the promise of Christ into the assurance of a glorious salvation. Our salvation depends, not on our good deeds, nor on our own righteousness; but upon the Word and the righteousness of the Lord Jesus Christ, and it is brought to us by faith in Him as our Saviour and King.

Not all will be saved

The request of the thief who repented, "Remember me when thou comest into thy kingdom", was not the only prayer that was prayed that day; for the thief on the other cross also made a request. He, we are told, railed on Jesus saying, "If thou be Christ, save thyself and us" (Luke 23 : 39). It appears that he had some kind of faith, believing that Jesus was not an ordinary person, for he asked Him, "Art not thou the Christ?" (R.V.). The very words he used suggest that he knew that Jesus was unique and therefore he asked Him to save both Himself and them. This prayer was understandable from one who was suffering so much; but it was a prayer that was limited. He was more concerned with physical survival than with his soul or his future destiny. Neither did he want a Saviour who died on a cross, but one who would step down from the cross and avoid the suffering and anguish of such a death.

Many people acknowledge the cross in some vague way, but they feel uncomfortable when they think about it, and do not want to hear about the blood of the Lord Jesus Christ. Some, like this thief, want the benefits that Christ gives, but not Christ Himself. One writer has expressed it in this way: "The appeal of this malefactor was on a level with an effort to break from prison". Just as a criminal might try to break out from prison, so this man in his last hour wanted to break away from his desperate plight. There seemed no thought in his mind of being rightly related to God, or of repenting of his sin and changing his way of life. His concern was an extension of his earthly life, maybe in order to go on living just as he had done before.

It is easy to sympathise with those who wish to "ban the bomb". Who among us would not like to see the cessation of the arms race between rival nations? But we need to beware of reflecting the attitude of the second thief. Do we wish to live in peace, not in order to live our lives to the glory of God, but to continue living as we like, "fulfilling the desires of the flesh and the mind, and walking according

to the course of this world"? Very many demand the benefits
of a Christian civilisation, whilst rejecting the Lord Jesus
Christ Himself and refusing to admit His claims upon them.
It is right to be concerned for the well-being of our children
and the generations yet unborn, but there are even deeper
needs than physical survival to consider. Our relationship
to Jesus Christ, our status before a holy God, the ultimate
question of our eternal destiny, these are the most important
issues in life, and they are the ones most often neglected.
They were neglected by the second thief.

But the first thief was concerned with just these things.
His plea was not for physical deliverance for himself or for
the Lord Jesus. It may well be that he dimly saw that his
future well-being was now the vital issue, and that it was
inextricably bound up with the death of the Person on the
central cross. It has frequently been pointed out that when
the thieves were first impaled on their crosses both of them
reviled and railed on Jesus. Matthew says, "The thieves also,
which were crucified with him, cast the same in his teeth"
(chap. 27 : 44). But there was a change in one of the thieves.
His railing stopped when he realised his hopeless and lost
condition.

Doubtless he had heard Jesus pray, "Father, forgive them for
they know not what they do", and recognised a quality in His
bearing and a dignity in His dying that marked Him as altogether different from himself. He renounced his mockery and
even rebuked his fellow thief for his mockery, "Dost not thou
fear God, seeing thou art in the same condemnation? And we
indeed justly; for we receive the due reward of our deeds".
He had come to see that they were receiving what they
deserved; more than that, he saw something of the majesty
and justice of God. His question did not concern fear of
pain or death, but fear of God. Death in itself is not
as important as what happens to us after death. "It is

appointed unto men once to die, but after this the judgment" (Heb. 9 : 27).

This is the solemn fact we face; that we shall appear before the throne where God is enthroned in all His glory as judge —the God whom we have offended, whose laws we have trampled upon.

More than this, the dying thief began to perceive the innocence of Christ, for he confessed, "This man hath done nothing amiss". The realisation dawned upon him that the Lord was not on the cross because He deserved to be, but was there as the blameless and righteous One. It was not His sin which had taken Him there, but the sin of the world which was placed upon Him. "God hath made him to be sin for us" (2 Cor. 5 : 21).

From what he said to Jesus we can infer that the thief was conscious also of the sovereignty of the Lord—"Remember me when thou comest into thy kingdom". It is only a king who rules over a kingdom. It needed no small insight to appreciate the regality of Jesus at this moment while He died upon a cross. The only crown He had worn was roughly plaited of thorns, and His sceptre was a common reed. Yet under these conditions there was a regal authority about the Lord Jesus, something so majestic that the dying thief perceived that the inscription above His head was in actual fact the truth, "Jesus of Nazareth, King . . .".

The thief knew too in his dying hour that there is another life, and that this physical existence is not all. So he sought to secure for himself the consideration of One who would be in control of the affairs of the next life. The kingdom which he knew would come was not an earthly one, for the Lord Jesus was leaving the world, not entering into it. Jesus Himself had earlier taught His disciples, "My kingdom is not of this world" (John 18 : 36). This thief not only realised his own unworthiness and the innocence of Jesus, but he also recognised His sovereign authority, and caught a glimpse of His coming kingdom.

The nature of salvation

The answer given by the Lord Jesus Christ to the thief who repented indicates to us something of the nature of salvation. What kind of deliverance did He offer to this poor man?

Clearly it was a *personal salvation*. We see how intimate was the relationship between the Lord and the thief, "Verily I say unto thee, Today shalt thou be with me in paradise". "Thou . . . with . . . Me." It would be difficult to think of a moral disparity greater than that between the thief and the Son of God. The thief—a robber, brigand and murderer, and the Lord Jesus Christ—the spotless Lamb of God; these were as far apart as any two could ever be. Yet they were together in their experience of the cross, and the Lord promised that they would be together too in paradise. What had they in common? Nothing, except the sin of one which was borne by the other. The moment the poor thief repented of his sin and cried for mercy, he began to experience a personal relationship with the Lord Jesus Christ. This is of the essence of salvation. It consists of a union between a person who repents of sin and the Lord Jesus Christ who redeems from sin. We are brought into the kingdom of God through putting our trust wholly in His Son.

Salvation is not only a personal experience shared by an individual and the Lord Jesus Christ, but also salvation is a *present experience*. The thief knew that Jesus had a kingdom; he wished to enter this kingdom, but he was not sure when and where it would be. He did not hesitate about the possibility of there being a kingdom, but he was cautious concerning when it would be established, "When thou comest into thy kingdom . . .". In other words he said, "I don't know when your kingdom will come, but, when it does come, please Lord remember me". Our Lord's reply was immediately reassuring, "Verily I say . . . Today shalt thou be with me". This is an experience which can be entered into now. It is the wonder of the gospel that it does not postpone our acceptance with God until we are fit to be accepted. If we were put on probation until we were worthy none of us would ever be accepted. Nor could we ever experience conversion if it depended upon our own ability to change ourselves.

"The men of grace have found glory begun below." The dying thief was not only going to heaven, but heaven was brought to him. There upon the cross a new hope arose in his heart, a new life, eternal not physical, surged through his personality.

"The vilest offender who truly believes
That moment from Jesus a pardon receives."

This present personal salvation is also a *perfect salvation,* for the Lord's promise was of paradise. What does this word paradise mean to us? Perhaps it takes our thoughts back to the first chapters of the Bible, to the garden of Eden, reminding us of beauty, fruitfulness, enjoyment and plenty. That first paradise was lost through man's sin, but there is another paradise where light and glory shine. Heaven is far more wonderful than the first earthly paradise. It is open to all who truly repent and believe on the Lord Jesus Christ. Any who cry to Him, as did the dying thief, can rest upon His promise and be assured that he will enter upon a larger, fuller, glorious life with God, and with His Son, in company with all the saints who throughout the ages have put their trust in the Lord Jesus Christ.

Let an old preacher sum it up for us then, as he says, " 'Today,' what speed; 'with me,' what company; 'in paradise,' what repose, what felicity."

III. BEHOLD THY SON

"When Jesus therefore saw his mother, and the disciple standing by, whom he loved, he saith unto his mother, Woman behold thy son! Then saith he to the disciple, Behold thy mother! And from that hour that disciple took her unto his own home."

John 19: 26-27.

The third time that Jesus spoke from the cross He expressed His compassionate concern for Mary, His mother. Around the cross many voices could be heard. Among them the taunting voices of the chief priests, the voices of the Roman soldiers who chattered and gambled among themselves, the mumbling mob who jeered and scoffed at a crucifixion, as they would at a carnival. But there were other voices too, hushed and solemn, coming from another smaller group standing apart from the rest. Most of this group were women and included Jesus' own mother. John was the sole disciple amongst them. We could count up to four or five women there, but only one man.

More often than not women show a greater devotion to Jesus Christ than do men. In many of our congregations their loyalty is evident; and of the prayer meetings in our churches it has been said, "They were started by brethren, but are maintained by sisters". An emasculated gospel preached from the pulpit does nothing to attract men, and is a far cry from the challenging, demanding message which Jesus Christ preached to men whilst here on earth. But it remains true that, as at the cross, so in our day, godly women often eclipse men in their dedication and discipleship.

Our Lord was comforted in the hour of His greatest need to know that one group of people near the cross was not there to scoff at Him, but because in their love and loyalty they wanted to be near, sharing with Him, as much as they could, the shame of His death. He looked down, as best He could, from the cross and spoke for the last time to His mother. As far as we know He did not speak to her again after His resurrection, as He did to Mary Magdalene and others of the disciples. What He said was simple, remarkable, not so much for what He did say, as for what He left unsaid. He offered no explanation of His sufferings. He did not relieve Mary's anxiety by explaining the deeper meaning of the cross, nor talk to her of heaven or the house of many mansions. None of these things was mentioned in the short sentence He spoke to her. He had one, very practical, thing to say. Unable to give any signal, save perhaps with His eyes, He directed her attention to the one disciple standing with her, "Woman, behold thy son". From now on Mary was to have another son in His place to take care of her and love her. Then He spoke to John, without even calling him by his name, "Behold thy mother"—"Woman, behold thy son . . . son, behold thy mother".

In order to impress this scene upon our minds, it may help to remember that there were three people involved in this third word from the cross. They were the Lord Jesus Christ, Mary, His earthly mother, and the disciple whom Jesus loved.

Mary, by the cross

"Now there stood by the cross of Jesus Mary his mother." What a remarkable person she was, highly favoured among women, yet her life was marked by sorrow and heartbreak. The greatest honour that could be bestowed upon a human being was bestowed upon Mary; her body was made to be the temple of God, and brought forth into this world the Saviour. No greater honour could she have known, yet with it came great sorrow and tragedy.

From the beginning Mary knew sorrow. When Gabriel appeared and told her that she was to be the mother of Jesus, she was troubled at his saying. Have we considered the shadow that hung over Mary from that day on? No other child had entered the world in this way. "The Holy Ghost shall come upon thee, and the power of the Highest shall overshadow thee . . . also that holy thing which shall be born of thee shall be called the Son of God" (Luke 1 :35). Joseph could not understand it until in a dream he was reassured. Many people did not accept the story of the angel, as there are those today who do not believe in the virgin birth. The religious leaders of our Lord's time actually went as far as to affront Him by saying that He was born of fornication. All through her life, though pure in morals and thought, Mary bore the stigma that such a miraculous conception involved.

When as a babe Jesus was taken into the temple, Simeon took Him up in his arms and made this prophecy, "Behold, this child is set for the fall and rising again of many in Israel; and for a sign which shall be spoken against; (Yea, a sword shall pierce through thy own soul also)" (Luke 2 : 34-35). He foretold her great anguish, which she would suffer as the mother of this child. When Jesus began to grow up, Mary did not understand Him, although He was her own son. When, as a child of twelve, she found Him in the temple among the doctors of the law, she gently chided Him, "Son why hast thou thus dealt with us? behold thy father and I have sought thee sorrowing" (Luke 2 : 48). Neither Mary nor Joseph understood the answer He gave to them.

When He preached His first sermon in Nazareth we can

imagine with what eagerness Mary would listen to Him in the synagogue on the sabbath day, where the rest of the family would be gathered with their neighbours and the other inhabitants of the town. The sermon began helpfully, and the people were attracted by the gracious words which fell from His lips; but then He began to apply His message. He reminded them of how Elijah, one of their greatest prophets, had to go to the country of Jezebel in order to get lodging, for no one in Israel would entertain him. He told them of the many lepers in the days of Elisha, of whom not one was cleansed, whilst Naaman the Syrian, who believed the prophet of God, was healed. This indictment was too pointed for them to tolerate, so with murder in their hearts, they led Him out to the brow of a hill and tried to throw Him over (Luke 4 : 21-29). Our Lord passed through the crowd and went on His way; but we can appreciate the dismay in Mary's heart, as she went home that day from the synagogue.

As Jesus continued going about His Father's business, Mary and the other members of the family became more and more alarmed. On one occasion His brothers began to think that He was deranged. On another, His mother with His brothers tried to intervene in His activities; "While he yet talked to the people, behold his mother and his brethren stood without, desiring to speak with him" (Matt. 12 : 46). While Mary pondered what Jesus was doing, and what people were saying about Him, it must have increasingly dawned upon her that God's hand was upon Him, and that He was indeed the Messiah, the suffering servant, whose path was leading to the cross.

Ultimately the hatred of the religious leaders became manifest, the common people were influenced to turn against Him, and He was led in derision and ignominy to the cross. Here the sword pierced most deeply into Mary's soul. Now she watched her first-born—so particularly precious—as He hung on the cross. She had been the first to place a kiss upon His brow, but now it was crowned with thorns. She was the first to guide His little feet and lead Him as a child, now those hands and feet were nailed to the cross. The fact that she was standing there shows how deeply she was involved in His death. The strong chains of love bound her to Him.

It is moving to read that Mary *stood* by the cross. She did not faint or collapse in the anguish of this experience. In reverent dignity, but great sorrow of heart, Mary stood near to her dying son.

Jesus, on the cross

Our Lord could see His mother from the cross. He did not need to be told of her feelings; He knew of the sword that was piercing her soul. He had something to say to her. It is significant that His half-brothers and sisters, Mary's other children, were not there. That He had such brothers and at least two sisters we are clearly told. He was the first-born son of Mary; but there were others born after Jesus. In Mark 6 : 3 we read that the people said, "Is not this the carpenter, the son of Mary, the brother of James, and Joses, and of Juda, and Simon? and are not his sisters here with us?" Yet, although there were four brothers and at least two sisters, Mary was at the cross alone. It seems probable from the silence of Scripture that Joseph had died some years earlier. Mary was at the cross as a widow, and was the only member of the family to witness the death of Jesus.

What had our Lord to say to her? Her greatest need at that moment was someone to comfort her and care for her. Jesus Himself could no longer exercise the responsibilities of the eldest son, so He gave her over to the care of John. He did not ask John to take her to one of His brothers or sisters to be looked after by them. It may have been that there was an estrangement in the family, and that Mary was the only one to believe that Jesus was the Messiah. For John tells us plainly in his gospel, "Neither did his brethren believe on him".

The Lord Jesus during His ministry gave a warning about the cost of discipleship, in particular the barriers it may set up within the family. He said, "A man's foes shall be they of his own household" (Matt. 10 : 36). Within his own family a man may find great opposition because of his loyalty to the Lord Jesus Christ. This can happen however considerate a man may be. On another occasion Jesus said, "Think not that I am come to send peace on the earth: I came not to send peace but a sword" (Matt. 10 : 34). He did not imply a physical sword, but the very real and distressing conflict which can come into a family when one member is converted and seeks to follow Him. This is especially the case with Jewish or Moslem believers, who are invariably disowned by their family when they become Christian. When Jesus said, "A man's foes shall be they of his own house" He knew it from experience, for His own brothers did not believe in Him. He could not therefore commit Mary to their care, and so He committed her to the care of John, the disciple whom He loved, and who loved Him.

It is not without interest to notice the way in which the Lord addressed Mary. John makes it plain to us that Mary was the mother of Jesus, "There stood by the cross of Jesus his mother" . . . "He saith unto his mother" . . . "When Jesus therefore saw his mother." At least four times John uses the word mother. Yet when the Lord spoke to her He did not call her mother. He said, "Woman, behold thy son." His restraint in speaking to her is very important.

We must not imagine that there was any harshness in the term "woman", although it may sound strange to our ears. In the language used by our Lord it would have the same meaning as our word "lady", or "madam". It is in effect a title of deference, honour and respect; but it is not the term we would expect a son to use when speaking to his mother. The Lord was giving comfort to Mary and making provision for her future care. Would it not have rejoiced her heart had He called her mother? But He did not, He spoke to her as "madam".

Throughout the gospel records there is not a single occasion when the Lord Jesus publicly called Mary "mother". He was always restrained in His choice of words when speaking to her. It is certain that no one can use His attitude to Mary as an argument to support Mariolatry. The extravagant titles ascribed to Mary, such as "Queen of Heaven", "Mother of God" and "Mother of the Church", and the prayers and homage paid to her are in singular contrast to our Lord's simple, almost severe, and yet polite, attitude and words to her.

Highly favoured among women, Mary herself was conscious of her privileged position of being the mother of the Lord Jesus. In the Magnificat she sang, "My spirit doth rejoice in God my Saviour". She, like any other, was saved by the merit of the Lord Jesus Christ alone. It seems as though on the cross our Lord was gently severing their human relationship altogether. In His words, "Woman behold your son, . . . son behold your mother", is there not the suggestion that He was no longer her son, that now John had undertaken this responsibility to her? A spiritual relationship of Saviour and saved was established at the cross which superceded and overshadowed their human relationship of son and mother.

Our Lord was thus setting us an important example. One of the ten commandments binding upon us concerns our attitude to our parents, "Honour thy father and thy mother" (Exod. 20 : 12). This is brought again to our notice by the apostle Paul, "Children, obey your parents in the Lord"

(Eph. 6 : 1). In the hour of His death the Lord perfectly exemplified this precept. He honoured His mother by making arrangements for her future care.

Christian children ought always to honour their parents, and when no longer under their immediate authority, ought to follow the example of the Lord Jesus and give the honour, love and help that they need and deserve. One of the tragedies of our age is the disrespect shown by many young people to their parents, and even at times the callous neglect of ageing relatives. Such is the antithesis to the teaching and example of the Lord Jesus Christ. Even when in physical agony upon the cross, He was still mindful of His responsibility to His mother.

In fulfilling His duty to Mary, Jesus shows us that our relationship to God does not mean that we can ignore our personal responsibilities. In our service for God we must not neglect human ties. Consider what the Lord Jesus Christ was accomplishing—the atonement for the world's sin. This was the mightiest event ever to take place. Yet in this hour He did not forget the practical needs of one person. His words to her were not, "I am so engaged in this mighty work of the world's redemption, that I am unable to concern myself with lesser matters". Nor did He at this moment talk to her of the house of many mansions she would occupy in the next life. On the contrary He made practical arrangements which would help her in the immediate heart-breaking hours and days following His death, "From that hour that disciple took her unto his own home".

There is a magnificent balance in the teaching of Jesus Christ. We should do well to "set the Lord always before us", and follow not only His doctrine but His practical example as well. There is a danger of our becoming unbalanced in our discipleship, which we may avoid if we seek the whole counsel of God. It is a wrong conception of the

Christian life, and Christian service, which would lead us to think that we can ignore our responsibilities towards our fellow human beings, so long as we think we are serving God. Whilst we should strive to be of service in the house of God and to His people, and not neglect them for our own home and personal interests, we should not neglect our home and family life. Paul, the great servant of God, tells us that we need to practise piety first at home. Our spiritual relationship to the Lord does not exempt us from our human relationships and responsibilities. Rather it should make us more sensitive to them, and more conscientious in our discharge of them.

John, near the cross

How near John was to the cross of the Lord Jesus Christ we do not know; but we know that he, the disciple whom Jesus loved, was standing alongside Mary with the small group who were there, not in derision or hatred, but because they truly loved Him. The way in which he describes himself does not imply that Jesus loved John more than He loved His other disciples; but John did seem to have a greater capacity to appreciate the love of Jesus. It was he who leaned on Jesus' breast as they ate their last meal together. John seems to be telling us his experience, in effect, "I don't know what others have experienced of Jesus Christ; but, so far as I am concerned, such has been His grace towards me that He has shown that He loves me. This is my testimony, I am a disciple whom Jesus loves".

The fact that John was standing near the cross proves that the love of Jesus had taken effect in his life. He, with all the other disciples on the night of our Lord's betrayal, forsook Him and fled away. They had been forewarned of their failure, "All ye shall be offended because of me this night" (Matt. 26 : 31). Quite categorically we are told that they all

forsook Him and fled, and that included John. But the love
that Jesus had shown him was strong enough to overcome
his fear, and John turned back and followed Jesus into the
courtyard of the high priest's house. He could no longer
stay away and so, through the long dark hours that followed,
he stayed as near as he could to the Lord. He took after Him
the road to the cross, and on top of the hill of Calvary he
stood nearby while Jesus was crucified.

You may in your Christian life have lapsed from a close
walk with the Lord Jesus Christ. If this has happened you
will have discovered, like John, that the only place where
you can find true joy and blessing is at the side of Jesus
Christ. However far you may have wandered away from
Him, come back to where He is; He will receive you in His
grace, He will heal your back-slidings and He will love you
freely. That He did so with John is seen by the task that He
committed to him. He entrusted him with something that He
was no longer able to do Himself. He entrusted Mary to his
care and protection.

The Lord Jesus Christ is now in glory, where He ascended
after arising from the dead. He is "seated at the right hand
of God". The church of Jesus Christ on earth—those whom
He has redeemed by His blood, and called to be His own—
is spoken of as the "body of Christ". They are the people
through whom He now does His work in the earth, "Now
ye are the body of Christ, and members in particular" (1 Cor.
12 : 27). All who are joined to Him in His risen life are
commissioned by Him, "As my Father hath sent me, even
so send I you" (John 20 : 21).

The Lord Jesus took our place on the cross, was our
substitute and was made sin for us. This was something He
alone could do; the only contribution we could make to the
cross was the sin that made His death necessary. But, as
redeemed sinners, He lifts us into fellowship with Himself,

and calls us to be His representatives in this world. How elevated our service becomes when we remember this. Think of entering a house and caring for someone who is ill or needy, and doing it in the name of Jesus as His representative. Think of witnessing at an open-air service, of visiting the sick in hospital, and doing it in the name of the Lord Jesus, as His ambassador. He has entrusted His work to His people here on earth. It has not been committed to the angels, but to those of us who belong to Him, as it was to John at the cross.

This is not the last time we read of John and Mary. Later we find them in a far different situation, in the upper room where Mary and Jesus' brothers were with other disciples awaiting the descent of the Holy Spirit, whom Jesus had promised to send to be their Guide and Comforter. All the disciples who were still faithful to their Lord—one hundred and twenty of them—were all "with one accord in one place".

This is the last time that we read of Mary, Jesus' mother, and we immediately notice that she was not alone. "Mary the mother of Jesus, and . . . his brethren" (Acts 1 : 14). Her other sons came to believe in the Lord Jesus Christ, and the family was united in devotion to Him. Perhaps Mary's stay at the home of John was not a very long one after all! The last picture we have of Mary is not that of a woman who sustained a particular relationship to the Lord Jesus Christ, exalting her above all other women. She is just a believer amongst other believers, who are praying together, giving praise and glory to God, and waiting for the Holy Spirit to empower them to go out and witness to their faith in the Lord Jesus Christ.

IV. FORSAKEN

"And about the ninth hour Jesus cried with a loud voice saying, Eli, Eli, lama sabachthani? that is to say, My God, my God, why hast thou forsaken me?"
Matthew 27:46.

This was our Lord's cry of dereliction from out of the darkness, "My God, my God, why hast thou forsaken me?"

How can the darkness be explained?

Why should there be such darkness? It was not midnight but midday, and the sun should have been blazing at its zenith of light and heat. Did the darkness come gradually, gently as a twilight, or was it a sudden, startling blotting-out of the light? We are not told how it came, only that it did come.

That darkness cannot be explained in terms of natural phenomena, such as an eclipse of the sun. As it was the time of the passover, there would have been a full moon at night and there cannot be an eclipse of the sun at the time of full moon. Luke tells us "the sun was darkened". The ninth of the ten plagues that came upon Egypt before the exodus of God's people was a plague of thick darkness which covered the land for three days (Exod. 10 : 22). The darkness which came whilst Jesus was on the cross lasted, we are told, for three hours—three hours of total darkness around midday. Imagine the shock, the fear and trembling of those on the hill of Calvary. The jeering and laughter would be replaced by a strange disquiet and unrest, as the people were shrouded

39

in uncanny darkness, broken only by the groans of the victims upon their crosses. This was something supernatural.

What does the darkness represent?

It would seem as if all nature was in protest against the injustice being done to the Son of God. To many He was Jesus of Nazareth, the son of a village carpenter and a wandering preacher; but, in the mystery of the gospel, He is also the everlasting Son of God, the co-creator of the world, man's Maker (John 1 : 1-3).

Matthew describes the other things that happened later, the earthquake, the graves of those who had believed in God opened and the corpses coming forth from their entombment. Nature itself shook in sympathy with the indescribable sufferings of the Son of God.

> *"Well might the sun in darkness hide*
> *And shut its glories in,*
> *When Christ the mighty Maker died,*
> *For man, the creature's sin."*

But the darkness was more than a protest, it was a symbol of the judgment of God upon sin. "God is light, and in him is no darkness at all" (1 John 1 : 5). In the Scriptures sin is often correlated with darkness, holiness with light. It is an obvious fact that many evil deeds, many iniquities are perpetrated under cover of darkness. John observes that there are many who refuse to come out in the open because they do not want their evil behaviour to be revealed (John 3 : 19-20). We have but to recall for a moment the underworld night life of any big city, or what goes on in many a village or town—the crime, thieving and immorality which take place under the pall of darkness.

A darkness covered the base evil enacted on Calvary, and it symbolised God's judgment on sin. Spurgeon suggests that the physical darkness was but a symbol of a deeper, more real darkness, which is called in the New Testament "outer darkness", where there is weeping and gnashing of teeth.

Towards the end of the three hours of darkness, as it began to lift, Jesus made a tremendous utterance. "About the ninth hour (three o'clock in the afternoon) Jesus cried with a loud voice saying, My God, my God, why hast *thou* forsaken me?"

It is impossible to forget the words of God to Moses at the burning bush, "Take off thy shoes from off thy feet, for the ground whereon thou standest is holy ground" (Exod. 3 : 5). We cannot do more than walk into the shallows of this verse. We can never hope to plumb the ocean depths of its meaning. This cry is as deep as God Himself, as deep as the bottomless pit, as deep as the awfulness of sin, as deep as the deep, deep love of Jesus. "My God, why hast *thou* forsaken me?"

Was the Lord Jesus forsaken by God?

Could it be true that He was really forsaken by His Father? Many have tried to explain the meaning of this cry.

Some say that Jesus was mistaken, that He thought that God had forsaken Him, but that in reality God was with Him all the time. As John the Baptist, in a moment of depression and doubt alone in Herod's prison cell, began to wonder whether Jesus Christ truly was the promised Messiah, so Jesus, because He was human, temporarily lost His confidence in God. In terrifying isolation He felt that even God had forsaken Him. But this cannot be the meaning of these words. This was the most important moment in the life of Jesus Christ—the moment for which He had been preparing Himself from the foundation of the world, before man was created, before man had sinned. "Known unto God are all his works from the very beginning" (Acts 15 : 18). The Lord Jesus Christ was on the cross in God's eternal purpose for the redemption of a fallen world. Is it likely that at this, the most important moment in history, the Lord Jesus Christ should be mistaken?

Others have suggested that Jesus wanted solace and comfort in His suffering. As at other times words of Scripture came to His mind and, trying to comfort Himself, He began to recite Psalm 22, "My God, my God, why hast thou forsaken me?" But the pain was so great that He became delirious and faint, and could not continue. In Matthew's record, however, we can discover no point at which Jesus was delirious or faint. His mind was clear and lucid from the beginning of His suffering until the last moment, when He dismissed His spirit and entered again into eternity. He cried with a loud voice—it was almost a shout of affirmation, not a murmuring plea of doubt. It is true that Jesus was fulfilling the prophecy concerning Himself in Psalm 22; but that is an altogether different subject.

We are brought to this conviction, that the only adequate explanation of the verse is that the Lord Jesus was actually forsaken by His Father at this moment. There is no sadder word in our language than the word "forsaken". I think of a widow who has returned from the funeral of her beloved husband. She has no other relative, no friends; as she walks through a cold empty house alone, she is forsaken. I think of a child whose parents have been killed in a road accident. Until help comes and a friendly hand is stretched towards him, he is alone, forsaken. To be forsaken by those we love is a fearful experience; but what is it compared with being forsaken by God in the hour of greatest need? Jesus in His greatest hour of need was forsaken by God, cast out from the loving presence of His Father.

Jesus knew what it felt like to be forsaken by men, it had happened to Him all too often. His relations misunderstanding Him, even thinking that He was deranged, forsook Him.

His fellow Nazarenes took Him up the hill to push Him over the top, and would have done so had they the power. The city of Jerusalem, the city of the great king, forsook Him, making Him weep at their indifference. His own nation whom He had come to redeem forsook Him. At the last as He faced arrest and trial and execution His nearest, His disciples, forsook Him and fled away (Matt. 26 : 56). Despite all this Jesus was comforted, "Ye shall be scattered, every man to his own, and shall leave me alone; and yet I am not alone, because my Father is with me" (John 16 : 32). He then had the tender, healing communion with His Father. But now, at last, He is forsaken of God!

In His other prayers from the cross the Lord Jesus said "Father"—"Father forgive them", "Father into Thy hands I commend my spirit". But now He says not, "My Father, my Father, why hast thou forsaken me?"—but, "My God, my God . . .".

It is a wonderful thing, an amazing thing that Jesus Christ should ever have left heaven to come into this world. Think of His infinite condescension, stepping down from a realm of glory, from the presence of His Father and the holy angels, to come through the womb of a Jewish village girl into the stream of humanity, into a world of hatred and greed and envy. Coming under the law of God, made lower than the angels in order to suffer death; yet even this great act of humility did not sever the fellowship between Him and His heavenly Father. It was not so immediate: He was no longer in heaven as it were at His Father's side, yet it was just as intimate. He could say, "The Father hath not left me alone, for I do always those things that please him" (John 8 : 29). Throughout His earthly life He was constantly in touch with His Father. At Lazarus' grave He said, "Father I thank thee that thou hast heard me. And I know that thou hearest me always" (John 11 : 41-42).

From all eternity God the Father and God the Son were in fellowship with one another, until this dreadful moment. Their unique communion was clouded and broken, bringing from Jesus these agonising words, "My God, my God, why . . .?"

Going out from a brilliantly lit room into a dark night, the darkness is all the more black by contrast. The Lord Jesus had basked in the light and glory of His Father's presence; but now on the cross He is plunged into the darkness, the blackness of desolation and abandonment.

Why was the Lord Jesus forsaken of God?

Martin Luther set himself to study this verse. He fasted, spoke to no one and was as if in a trance. For several hours he did not move, then he got up from his chair to walk around the room. He was overheard saying, "God forsaken of God? Who can understand that?" This is why we can only wade in the shallows of what this verse means. The Lord Jesus Christ was God, manifest in the flesh. God manifest in the flesh, yet forsaken of God. Who indeed can understand that?

At this point, however, the Lord Jesus was our representative, our substitute, our mediator and sin-bearer. We can only begin to understand the meaning of His words by first of all recognising *the character of God*. God is love, but He is holy love, pure love, "Thou art of purer eyes than to behold evil, and canst not look upon iniquity" (Hab. 1 : 13). Don't try to whittle this down! God is so holy that the angels who have never sinned are in awe of His holiness. Theirs is a derived holiness, a pale reflection of the essential eternal holiness of God. In His presence they veil their faces, cover their feet and cry, "Holy, holy, holy, is the Lord of hosts" (Isa. 6 : 3). The holiness of God is such that no man could dare to look into His face. When the Lord Jesus took on

Himself the world's sin, it was impossible for God to gaze upon Him or to speak with Him.

God who is holy is also just. Justice must put limits upon injustice; these limits we call laws, and God's justice is expressed in His laws against sin. "The wages of sin is death" (Rom. 6 : 23). Death here means more than mere cessation of physical life, it means separation, not merely from life, but from God Himself. To die this death is to be where the footsteps of God's mercy never fall. Everyone of us has broken the laws of God, everyone is under sentence of death— "Cursed is everyone that continueth not in all things which are written in the book of the law to do them" (Gal. 3 : 10). The purpose of the Lord Jesus Christ's death upon the cross was to pay the penalty for us. He, the sinless One, became sin for us and fulfilled the law to its total demand, therefore making it unnecessary for us to die for our lawlessness and sin. "For God hath made him to be sin *for us,* who knew no sin" (2 Cor. 5 : 21): "Christ hath delivered us from the curse of the law, being made a curse *for us*" (Gal. 5 : 21).

Until we grasp in some measure the character of God, that He is holy and just in His love, we cannot begin to understand the full meaning of Christ's forsakenness upon the cross.

Neither can we appreciate it unless we know something of the purpose of Christ's death. He did not die as a martyr; that, perhaps, would have brought about His own salvation, but it could not save anyone else. He did not die merely as a good example; an example is meant to be followed and copied, but it can never achieve pardon for sin, or release a man from the dominion and power of sin. He died there for us, as our substitute, our representative. "He was wounded for our transgressions, he was bruised for our iniquities" (Isa. 53 : 5).

In an Old Testament book, Leviticus, in chapter 16 we read of a scapegoat. The goat was brought to the door of the tabernacle where the Hebrew people worshipped God; the people gathered around Aaron, their high priest; he put his hands on the goat and at the same time confessed all the sins of the people. Symbolically he was transferring all the sins of the people on to the goat, which was then led away far into the wilderness to a place of desolation, where it wandered until its death and was seen no more. The Lord Jesus Christ became our "scapegoat", our sins were transferred to Him and He bore them away into isolation and dereliction.

Sin is a loathsome thing to us when we are in our right minds. How much more loathsome is it to God the holy One. When Christ was loaded with the sin of the whole world He was separated by it from God. He had no light, for God is light; He felt no love, for God is love. He was outside the light and love of God, abandoned as the scapegoat in a place of dereliction.

His cry was the cry of a sinking soul, sinking without any possibility of support. Sinking, sinking, sinking as if to depths without end. Elizabeth Clephane in the hymn, "There were ninety and nine . . .", has expressed it in these words:

"But none of the ransomed ever knew
How deep were the waters crossed;
Nor how dark was the night that the Lord passed through
Ere He found His sheep that was lost."

What can we learn from this cry?

First and foremost it teaches us the greatness of the love of God and of the Lord Jesus Christ. This was the greatest display of love the world could ever know. How greatly God must love us, to give up His Son to this ignominy, this shame, this appalling anguish. "For God *so* loved the world that he gave his only begotten Son" (John 3 : 16). In the mystery of God, both Father and Son were in this together. We know that God had as it were to turn His face away from Jesus when He was made sin for us, yet at that very moment the Lord Jesus was doing the will of God, and in doing His will was one with Him. "For God was in Christ reconciling the world unto himself" (2 Cor. 5 : 19). And how greatly Jesus loved us, being prepared to go through with the condemnation of sin upon Himself. "Having loved his own . . . he loved them unto the end" (John 13 : 1).

This surely must teach us also the enormity of sin. If anyone thinks of sin as trivial, as something that can easily be remedied or removed, let him turn again to the cross. This is the end product of sin, this is its price, this is the only way in which it can be dealt with. The measure of what Jesus endured upon the cross is the measure of sin. Its enormity is beyond our comprehension.

There is too, in this cry, a warning. Jesus suffered the penalty of sin. That penalty is hell, torment, the wrath of God—and what these mean we can hardly imagine. But they are the words of the Scriptures and are grave warnings to us.

Because the Lord Jesus Christ was the Son of God He doubtless had a greater capacity to feel and to endure the consequences of sin. Christian people may never know nor suffer to this extent.

> *"There lies beneath its shadow,*
> *but on the farther side,*
> *The darkness of an awful grave*
> *which gapes both deep and wide,*
> *And there between us stands*
> *the cross, two arms outstretched to save*
> *Like a watchman set to guard the way*
> *from that eternal grave."*

How much we need to think deeply and long on the tremendous cry of dereliction which came from our Lord's lips, as He hung there on the cross in the shrouding darkness. Do we meditate enough on what it cost our Lord to redeem our unworthy little lives? Do we ponder enough on this amazing display of God's love? How shamefully trivial much in our lives must look in comparison. Would that we knew more of the life of God in our souls, of His power in our lives and of communion with Him. "Think on these things."

If you are not a Christian, have you ever stopped to think seriously about what actually happened at that historical event of the crucifixion of Jesus Christ? Is it something you can dismiss lightly from your mind, something you can joke about or use in clever arguments and repartee? Think again of the enormity of sin in the sight of God. Should we not seek a way of escape from His wrath upon it: "For if the word spoken by angels was steadfast, and every transgression and disobedience received a just recompense of reward; how shall we escape, if we neglect so great salvation".

V. I THIRST

"After this, Jesus knowing that all things were now accomplished that the Scriptures might be fulfilled, saith, I thirst." John 19:28.

Throughout the long agonising hours that led up to this moment on the cross, the Lord Jesus Christ never once drew attention to Himself, nor enlisted the sympathy of the onlookers. The women who wept at His plight He told to weep not for Him, but for themselves, on account of what was later to befall them. This is the one exception where He acknowledges His feelings, and cries out with a loud voice, "I thirst".

It has been suggested that the Lord desired a drink to quench His thirst, and so be able to recruit all His strength for the final moments of His death, and that He might consciously and voluntarily commit Himself to His heavenly Father, and dismiss His own spirit from His body when He had completed what He set out to do. But we should note that He did not ask for a drink, but merely stated the fact of His condition. Did He expect any response to His words? We know that one of the men standing nearby brought some sour wine in a sponge and lifted it up on a rod to the mouth of the Lord. We know that our Lord accepted the wine, sucking it from the sponge.

What then do we learn from this incident? Let us consider some of its lessons:

The greatness of the suffering of the Lord Jesus Christ

Crucifixion is probably the most cruel and painful form of death. The pain it causes is both excruciating and prolonged. Our Lord was on the cross for six hours before He gave up His spirit. Others lived for much longer in that awful pain-racked suspension. The blood would gradually drain from the body, causing dehydration and increasing thirst. In Psalm 22 : 15 we read words which describe this experience, "My strength is dried up like a potsherd; and my tongue cleaveth to my jaws; and thou hast brought me into the dust of death".

The last time that the Lord drank prior to this was at the passover, when He shared His last meal with His disciples in the upper room, on the night on which He was betrayed. From the upper room He had walked to Gethsemane where He spent several hours in prayer, facing up to the implications of the cross, the bitter cup which He would drink, and in agony of spirit He sweated, as it were, great drops of blood. There followed His betrayal by Judas with a kiss as a mockery of friendship and discipleship, then His arrest, and in rapid succession four unjust trials. First He was brought before the high priest Caiaphas, then before Pilate, then He was hustled away to appear before King Herod, and then back again to Pilate.

The indignities the Lord Jesus Christ suffered can scarce be dwelt upon—the spitting in His face, the plucking of His beard, being arrayed in a mock-kingly robe and a crown (but one of thorns) placed upon His head. He was whipped; this in itself was so severe a punishment that prisoners were known to die under it. After all this He had to carry His own heavy cross, through the streets milling with the passover crowds, away to the place of execution. Stumbling under its weight He was, at last, helped by a bystander, who was forced

by the soldiers into taking one end of the cross for Him—one
solitary act of help in long hours of torment and cruelty.

Arriving at last on the hill of Calvary, Jesus, with the two
criminals, was forced to lie upon the cross. Their hands and
feet were nailed to their crosses. The crosses were then lifted
and jolted into the holes prepared for them in the ground,
the victims hanging in helpless agony above.

The Lord Jesus Christ who "knew no sin" would have a
sensitivity to pain beyond the sensitivity of an ordinary man.
Sin coarsens our human nature; but Jesus had not known
the effect of pride and hatred and evil, that blunts the con-
science and defiles the personality, and so He would feel
with full intensity the agony of pain and suffering. For three
hours the sun beat down relentlessly and a rabble of men,
women and children, spurred on by those with evil intent,
crowded around mocking, jeering and scoffing. For the next
three hours there followed that mysterious darkness, during
which the Lord was in a blackness of abandonment and
separation from His Father, weighed down with the sin of
the world. Isaiah tells us, "The Lord hath laid on him the
iniquity of us all" (chap. 53 : 6).

It was after the darkness had lifted, after He had paid the
penalty of sin, and the work of redemption was nearing its
completion that Jesus became aware of His own need and
cried out, "I thirst". It was almost the cry of one whose
victory is in sight.

It is difficult to use any human analogy to compare with
this experience; but one can imagine an athlete running in a
race, every nerve strained to its limit towards the winning
of the race. He reaches the tape, then at last, able to let up
a little from his tremendous effort, he becomes acutely
aware of the aches and pains in his limbs and muscles, and
his body cries out for rest and water. Or take another example
from the report of a road accident, in which two cars were in

severe collision. The driver of one of the cars was injured and blood began to stream down his face; but his wife and small son, more seriously injured, were unconscious. The man though injured walked to the nearest telephone to call for an ambulance and the police, then travelled with his wife and son in the ambulance sixty miles to hospital. His injuries were also treated and when discharged he returned to his home. Once there, he collapsed into bed and experienced a high fever. He had been able to carry on through many hours, his own pain in the background, until all necessary arrangements were made for the care of his wife and child; but when all was done he then realised his own condition.

The one consuming concern of the Lord Jesus Christ on the cross was the redemption of the world. He was there to bear the sins of the world, to do battle with the devil for the souls of men and, without minimising His suffering, we can say that this task was so all consuming that He had no thought for His personal sufferings.

> *"He had no tears for His own griefs,*
> *But shed drops of blood for mine."*

When the work neared its completion there was time for an awareness of His sufferings, and so He cried, "I thirst"—not in defeat, but as a victor exhausted in the battle. John writes, "After this, Jesus knowing that all things were now accomplished that the Scriptures might be fulfilled, saith, I thirst".

The humanity of the Lord Jesus Christ

This thought also emerges from this part of Christ's sufferings on the cross, that He is human as well as divine. The two natures were blended in perfection, all of God in His divine nature, all of man (apart from sin) in His human nature—a unique Being, no other like Him, nor ever will be. For God is God, and man is man, and neither can be the other. Yet God the Son through the womb of Mary became the Son of man, thus God and man in One.

As God, Jesus was with His Father, "In the beginning was the Word, and the Word was with God, and the Word was God" (John 1 : 1). He was God's agent in the creation of the world, "All things were made by him; and without him was not anything made that was made" (John 1 : 3). As a man, He was born a babe of Mary, He grew and learned and talked and laughed and cried—fully God, and fully man.

During our Lord's life and work on earth both sides of His Person were in evidence. As God He commanded Lazarus forth from the tomb; as man He wept for His friend. As man we see Him so weary that even the storm tossed sea did not awaken Him from sleep; as God we see Him stand to rebuke the wind and sea to an immediate calm.

On the cross we see God and man in Jesus Christ. We see God, as He offers immediate forgiveness and eternal life to a repentant criminal on another cross. We see man, as He thirsts. This is a mystery and a wonder of the gospel. We have One who is God and is therefore able to be to us a Saviour, but at the same time He is One who has experienced human weakness and limitations. Often in tragedy or bereavement people ask the question, "Why, if God is a God of love, does He allow this to happen?" The only possible answer to such a question is that God knows suffering too, that in His Son Jesus Christ He entered into human suffering to a degree greater than any other man. "In all their affliction he was afflicted" (Isa. 63 : 9). "He was touched with the feeling of our infirmities".

Our God is a God involved and identified with us; who is love, and love shown in His own suffering at Calvary. However sad our lot or tragic our circumstances, we have a God to whom we may turn, who is compassionate towards

us, who cares for us, who has come down into the midst of
our suffering and suffered more than we, in order to do away
with sin and give us new life.

> *"In every pang that rends the heart*
> *The Man of Sorrows has a part.*
> *He sympathises with our grief*
> *And to the sufferer sends relief."*

The fulfilment of Old Testament prophecies

The plain simple words, "I thirst", afford even further
proof if it were needed, that Jesus is indeed the Saviour of
the world. It is a remarkable thing about the crucifixion that
every event connected with it is predicted in the Old Testament, and each prediction is fulfilled accurately. John remarks
upon this fact again and again in his gospel, "These things
were done that the scripture should be fulfilled". One
example is seen in chapter 19 verses 34-37, where he says,
"But one of the soldiers with a spear pierced his side, and
forthwith came there out blood and water. And he that saw
it (that is John himself) bear record, and his record is true:
and he knoweth that he saith true, that ye might believe.
For these things were done, that the Scriptures should be
fulfilled. A bone of him shall not be broken. And again
another scripture saith, They shall look on him whom they
pierced."

Surely one of the greatest proofs of the inspiration of the
Bible is in the fulfilment of Old Testament prophecies. There
are too many, and they are too exact, to be dismissed or
ignored. Death by crucifixion was not known in Old Testament times. It was the brutal mode of capital punishment
introduced by the Romans. Yet David to whom it was un-
known, guided by the Holy Spirit, described the death of
the Messiah by this means. Then there is in the Messianic
Psalm 69, a reference to the Messiah's thirst (verse 21), which

we may compare with John 19 : 29, "Jesus . . . saith, I thirst".

We dare not imagine that Jesus was consciously fulfilling all the things which He could remember had been prophesied of His death. Such an idea would make Him little more than an actor acting out a drama. But John is so anxious to show that Christ is Messiah, that he emphasises this aspect of the crucifixion.

The background of these words

If we look at the records of this particular event in Matthew, Luke and John, we find that the Lord was offered drink before, during and at the end of the crucifixion. "And when they were come unto a place called Golgotha, that is to say, a place of a skull, they gave him vinegar to drink mingled with gall: and when he had tasted thereof, he would not drink" (Matt. 27 : 33-34). The offering of this strange drink was a humane act. It was a generally recognised narcotic and was offered to criminals in order to minimise to a small extent their sufferings during crucifixion. This drink the Lord refused.

He was prepared to face the full blast and onslaught of physical agony, and desired that His mind might be as clear and lucid as possible while He carried through the most tremendous work that had been predestined for Him from eternity. He received nothing that would act as a sedative to dull His faculties or lessen His pain as He took the world's sin upon Himself and paid the penalty it incurred.

During the first three hours upon the cross the soldiers made sport amongst themselves. Probably the fact that Jesus had refused the drink they had offered induced them to tantalise Him, and while He hung above them, they could drink their fill of their sour wine. "The soldiers also mocked him, coming to him and offering him vinegar" (Luke 23 :

36). Such is man's inhumanity to man. They taunted Him
with their wine, holding it up almost to His lips, then with-
drawing it in order to add to His afflictions. But soon the
strange darkness came upon the scene, subduing the taunts
and shielding the worst of Christ's sufferings from the shame-
less staring of men. Suffering His ultimate agony He cried
out, "My God, my God, why hast thou forsaken me?"

Then the darkness began to recede and very soon the Lord
yielded up His life. The next three things He said came in
quick succession. When He cried, "I thirst", a soldier came,
not now in derision, but with sincerity, and passed up a
sponge dipped in vinegar to the lips of the Lord Jesus.
Matthew suggests that he pressed the sponge to the lips of
Jesus again and again, so that He could drink and drink of
it. This appears as the one solitary act of kindness shown
by the crowds to the Lord Jesus through these long and painful hours. It would be heart-warming to think that this soldier
was showing signs of a change in his attitude to the Lord,
and that grace was working in his heart. It may be that to this
man Jesus has said, "I was thirsty and ye gave me drink".

There is a thirst other than a physical one. To the woman
at the well He said, "Give me to drink" (John 4 : 7). This
was His way of establishing a basis for conversation with her.
He may not have drunk any of the water she drew, but very
soon He was telling her of the water that He had to offer.
"If thou knewest the gift of God, and who it is that saith
to thee, Give me to drink; thou wouldst have asked of him,
and he would have given thee living water . . . whosoever
drinketh of this water shall thirst again: But whosoever
drinketh of the water that I shall give him shall never thirst;
but the water that I shall give him shall be in him a well of
water springing up into everlasting life" (John 4 : 10, 13-14).
When we come to Him and receive of Him the water of
life which He offers to us, it is then we drink of Him and

live, and know the experience of refreshment in the depths of our souls.

> *"I heard the voice of Jesus say,*
> *'Behold I freely give*
> *The living water; thirsty one,*
> *Stoop down and drink, and live.'*
> *I came to Jesus, and I drank*
> *Of that life-giving stream;*
> *My thirst was quenched, my soul revived,*
> *And now I live in Him."*

Horatius Bonar.

VI. FINISHED

"When Jesus therefore had received the vinegar, he said, It is finished."　　　　　　　　John 19:30.

This great proclamation, consisting of three words in our translation, is only one word in the original—"tetelestai". Literally it means "done".

The event is recorded in each of the four gospels. Matthew writes, "Jesus, when he had cried again with a loud voice, yielded up the ghost" (chap. 27:50). Mark writes, "And Jesus cried with a loud voice, and gave up the ghost" (chap. 15:37). In Luke we read, "And when Jesus had cried with a loud voice, he said, Father, into thy hands I commend my spirit: and having said this, he gave up the ghost" (chap. 23:46). The three writers tell us the way in which Jesus cried, "with a loud voice". They do not tell us what He cried; that John alone tells us, "It is finished". John was at the cross and heard for himself this great cry of triumph, when Jesus knew that His work of redemption was done.

There is something very significant about the fact that He cried "with a loud voice". It means that He was in perfect command of the situation. Though He had suffered so intensely, He was not languishing. This was a vigorous, clear cry of victory. It was loud enough for the angels in heaven to hear, and to set all heaven rejoicing to know that the work of redeeming a fallen creation, planned in eternity, had now been made actual in time. It was loud enough for the chief priests and scribes to hear, and to understand if they would that the old order was being replaced by the new. The sacrifices offered through the ages had now culminated in the perfect sacrifice for sin, and the way was opened into the holiest, the presence of God, for all men, through Jesus Christ our great High Priest. It is loud enough for men through all the world and through all ages to hear, and to know that the penalty for sin has been paid, and if they but turn to Jesus Christ in faith they may receive the gift of eternal life in Him.

The meaning of the cry

The Lord Jesus did not cry out, "I am finished". One might have expected that such suffering would at last have overwhelmed Him; but this was not so. Jesus was speaking, not of Himself, but of what He had been doing on the cross.

The crucifixion is often portrayed with the figure of Christ hanging upon the cross in utter weakness, a sight to claim our deepest sympathy. But this is not how the crucifixion ends in the New Testament. The Lord who died upon the cross did not remain on it. He yielded up His life, He was taken down from the cross and the cross was empty; it had been used by Christ, but now He had finished with it. He had hung there in weakness but even in His final moments of dying He was in perfect command of the situation. John tells us, "He bowed his head, and gave up the spirit" (chap. 19 : 30). Another translation is, "He dismissed his spirit". When He knew that the full penalty had been paid there was no longer need to remain upon the cross, and so He terminated His earthly life.

We have no such power, to will to die; we may say, "I wish to die", but we shall find ourselves still alive. This is different from suicide, which means killing ourselves by one of various methods. It is a voluntary cessation of earthly existence by yielding our life into the hands of God. We do not have the ability to do this, but the Lord Jesus did have such power;

so that He was not so much the victim of death, nor helplessly robbed of life, but rather the triumphant victor with power over life and death. When He knew His work on earth was complete, He gave up His life freely. Earlier He had Himself said, "I lay down my life . . . no man taketh it from me, but I lay it down of myself" (John 10 : 17-18).

This is an incomparable accomplishment with majestic meaning for us. It includes the fact that all His suffering and shame were finished. Isaiah describes our Lord as "A man of sorrows and acquainted with grief". He was born King, but He was also born to die. We are born to live, and though death comes to us all it is not the express purpose of our birth and life. But this was the purpose of our Lord's life. He came into the world in order that He might die for our sins. From the first His life was overshadowed by sorrow and suffering. At the age of twelve, when He was found in the temple in conversation with the doctors, He said to His mother, "Wist ye not that I must be about my Father's business?" (Luke 2 : 49). Even in Nazareth at the carpenter's bench, an idyllic life one could suppose, He knew that His task was to bring salvation to the world, that at thirty years of age He would step out on a ministry of suffering and affliction, which would culminate in the cross.

In a painting of Jesus as a young man the artist depicts Him in the carpenter's shop at Nazareth; He has been working hard at the bench and stretches out His hands to relax His muscles; the rays of the sun shining in through the open door cast a shadow of the body of Jesus upon the wall at the back of the workshop; the shadow is shaped like a cross. His mother looks in upon the scene and sees silhouetted upon the wall the shadow of the cross. Although this is only a picture, it is true that the shadow of Calvary hung over the entire life of the Lord Jesus Christ. When He stepped down into the waters of the river Jordan to be baptised by John, it was a committal of Himself to His life's work—the redemption of the world. The baptism in water was an anticipation of something more radical, the baptism in blood upon the cross, when all the waves and billows of God's wrath upon sin would flow over Him. It was not long after His baptism when John pointed Him out as, "The Lamb of God, which taketh away the sin of the world" (John 1 : 29).

That Jesus was conscious of His great call is shown by some of the things He said, almost as asides, on various occasions. When, at Caesarea Philippi, Peter confessed Him to be "The Son of the living God", at that significant moment Jesus told His disciples of the suffering and death which He would undergo (Matt. 16 : 21). On the mount of the transfiguration, when Moses and Elijah appeared, the very subject of their conversation with Jesus was the cross and the death which He should accomplish at Jerusalem (Mark 9 : 2-4). It is clear that from the beginning the Lord Jesus Christ was aware of His great destiny, that He had come into the world to be the Saviour of the world. Eventually we read of His betrayal into the hands of the Roman soldiers, of the injustice, derision and scorn poured upon Him, of the nails hammered into His hands and feet, of His endurance of the pangs and tortures of death upon the cross. Now that His destiny had been fulfilled, man had done his worst, the judgment of God upon sin had been carried out and Christ had met in full the condemnation, He could shout in triumph, "It is finished".

What the Lord had completed

This great affirmation means too that all the Old Testament prophecies concerning the life and death of the Lord Jesus Christ were fulfilled; they too were *finished*. In amazing detail the birth, life and death of Jesus are pre-intimated in the Old Testament, His birth (Isa. 7 : 14), where He would be born (Mic. 5 : 2), His escape into and return from Egypt

(Hos. 11 : 1), how He grew up and His suffering at the hands of men (Isa. 50 : 6), His death and resurrection (Isa. 53 : 12, Psa. 16 : 10); and other almost incidental things are mentioned which were all fulfilled in fact. John, as we have noticed, was especially aware of the way in which the Old Testament prophecies were fulfilled in the life and death of Christ.

There are two lines of prophecy running throughout the Old Testament. One tells of the first coming and life and death of the Lord Jesus Christ; the other line deals with His second coming. It was predicted that the One who was crucified upon the cross would be exalted to God's right hand, that He is coming again into the world to receive His own people to Himself, to judge the world in righteousness and to establish His everlasting kingdom. It is an encouragement to our faith to realise that every prophecy concerning our Lord's first coming into the world was fulfilled—finished. This is surely a guarantee that every prophecy concerning His second coming will also be fulfilled. "For yet a little while, and he that shall come, will come, and will not tarry" (Heb. 10 : 37).

"Finished" marks too the end of Old Testament rites, and the whole scheme of the priesthood and temple ceremonies. His sacrifice was finished, and, as it was the culmination of all the Old Testament sacrificial ceremonies, they too in this one sacrifice for sins for ever were *finished*.

Striking events took place when our Lord cried out these words, of which we read in Matthew 27, verses 50 and 51. "Jesus when he had cried again with a loud voice yielded up the ghost. And, behold, the veil of the temple was rent in twain from the top to the bottom; and the earth did quake, and the rocks rent." The massive curtain in the temple, veiling the "holiest of all" from the rest of the building, was ripped in half from the top to the bottom, signifying that the old order was finished. No longer was it necessary for the people to bring sacrifices to the priest, or for the priest on the day of atonement to go into the holiest of all with their offerings, for now the Lord Jesus Christ had offered Himself upon the cross as the full and final atonement for sin. The Old Testament sacrifices were a foreshadowing of His great sacrifice, they had no intrinsic value, as the writer to the Hebrews tells us, that "it is not possible that the blood of bulls and of goats should take away sins". The priestly sacrifices were a representation, a prefiguring of what was to come, having value only in so far as they pointed towards the actual event. They were like signposts pointing towards the future.

The New Testament makes it clear that there is no longer need for men to make material sacrifices as offerings to God for their sins, neither is an earthly priest required to perform this, which was his office during Old Testament times. "But this man after he had offered one sacrifice for sins for ever, sat down on the right hand of God" (Heb. 10 : 12). In Christ is a synthesis of all that went before, the altar, the sacrifice, the priesthood. He is now the one mediator between God and man, so there is no need for offerings, or ceremonies, or priests. Everyone who truly believes in Jesus Christ as his Saviour has direct access to God through Jesus Christ our great High Priest.

The cry of victory, "It is finished", heralded forth the good news that salvation was assured to all who would believe, for it was completed—*finished*. On the cross Christ was bearing the sins of all His people of all time. Their guilt was laid upon Him and He was paying their penalty. Not only was He offering Himself to His Father as the sinless Lamb, but in some mysterious way He was made sin. Beyond our comprehension is this fact that the whole mass of the world's sin was concentrated upon Him on the cross, and that the final consequences of that sin were exhausted upon Him. The Old Testament sacrifices were never complete. There was always need for more, and more, and more. Not one, or all of them together were enough to blot out the consequences of sin for ever. But the supreme sacrifice of Christ is enough. Instead of the fire of God's condemnation consuming the sacrifice as it did in the Old Testament, the sacrifice consumed, completely used up, the fire. The wrath of God upon sin was completely exhausted by the infinite value of the offering of Jesus Christ. His was a perfect, complete sacrifice to which nothing needed to be or could be added. All that God required to atone for sin was met. His righteousness had been satisfied.

> *"Jesus paid it all, all to Him I owe,*
> *Sin had left a crimson stain*
> *He washed it white as snow."*

There is nothing we can add

People are always wanting to do something towards their salvation. A letter I received some time ago explained why the writer felt no need to come to church. The reason he gave was that he was a regular contributor to the N.S.P.C.C., and he felt that this good work was enough to make him acceptable to God. Many people strive to live upright, respectable, law-abiding lives in order to be pleasing to God. Yet the teaching of the Bible is utterly plain. If we could be acceptable to God on account of our own good works, if they were enough to cancel out our guilt, there would have been no need for the Lord Jesus Christ to die at all. There is no do-it-yourself salvation. "Not by works of righteousness which we have done, but according to his mercy he saved us" (Tit. 3 : 5). There is nothing we can do, and nothing we can cease from doing, except repent and accept the offer of salvation from Jesus Christ. We must believe His gospel, trust in Him, the Lamb of God, who has paid the penalty of our sin for us willingly, freely, and for ever.

Many years ago a very earnest but somewhat unusual evangelist, by the name of Ebenezer Wooten, went about the rural areas of England preaching the gospel. On one occasion he was taking down his tent after conducting a series of meetings in a certain village (in those days the evangelist had to do almost everything himself) when a young man came to him and asked, "Mr. Wooten, what can I do to be saved?" Mr. Wooten was pulling up the tent stakes from the ground, and without looking up he said, "You are too late young man". The young man was rather taken aback and asked, "Do you mean that now the meetings are over I am too late to be saved?" "Oh no!" replied Mr. Wooten, "That is not what I mean; you asked, 'What can I do to be saved,' and my reply is that you are nineteen hundred years too late to do anything. The Lord Jesus did all that needed doing on the cross. All you need do is fall on your knees, repent and ask Jesus to receive you, trusting Him to be your Saviour." We were glad to read that the young man did just that.

That is all we can do. Have we done it? We can confess our sin and receive Jesus Christ as our Saviour and take our forgiveness from that which He completed upon the cross at Calvary when He cried, "It is finished". "Believe on the Lord Jesus Christ and thou shalt be saved" (Acts 16 : 31).

VII. INTO THY HANDS

"And when Jesus had cried with a loud voice, he said, Father into thy hands I commend my spirit."
Luke 23:46.

These are the last words which our Lord spoke from the cross. In all He spoke seven times, and to Jewish people seven was a number which had a special significance. It was associated with perfection or completion. Therefore to Jewish people the fact that Christ spoke seven times from the cross would imply that His words were in some way complete, they were not lacking, nor were there any superfluous words. Seven was also to Jewish people a number which signified rest, associated with the seventh day of creation when God rested, and with the sabbath day. Chapter 2 of Genesis begins, "Thus the heavens and the earth were finished, and all the host of them. And on the seventh day God ended his work which he had made; and he rested on the seventh day from all his work which he had made. And God blessed the seventh day, and sanctified it: because that in it he had rested from all his work which God created and made."

The work of the world's creation is comparable to the work of the world's redemption upon Calvary, except that redemption was far more costly a work for God to perform. The creation of the world was by the word of God, "For he spake and it was done, he commanded, and it stood fast" (Psa. 33 : 9). His word had the power of creation, "Let there be . . . and there was". But to redeem the world words were not enough, it could only be achieved by the blood and the death of the Son of God. Re-creation was costlier and

66

more demanding than the first creation. One writer has said that it would have been cheaper for God to make new creatures than for Him to re-make the old ones. There is truth in this, for He could have wiped out the whole of creation, which had fallen into sin and rebellion against Him, and begun again making a new race. But in spite of sin God loved the creatures He had made, "But God commendeth his love towards us, in that, while we were yet sinners, Christ died for us" (Rom. 5 : 8).

In creation the sixth day was the day on which God finished His work. On the cross the sixth cry was the triumphant cry, "Finished", which made heaven rejoice and hell tremble. Now follow the words of restfulness, the work all done Jesus commended Himself into the arms of His God, that He might rest there after His ordeal in accomplishing the amazing feat of the world's redemption.

"Father into thy hands I commend my spirit." These words reveal Jesus to us as the dependent Son of God. He yielded Himself to His Father's care and from that time on He went after His ascension to sit at the right hand of God in heaven, as the Son of the living God and the Mediator on the behalf of mankind for whom His redeeming work was performed.

The uniqueness of our Lord's death

His last words bring many thoughts into our minds. First is the fact of the uniqueness of our Lord's death. His use of the word "commend" is worthy of our notice. It means "lay down". In every account of His death in the gospels it is made quite clear that our Lord's death was voluntary. It was He Himself who finally decided the precise moment at which His death should come.

When Stephen was stoned to death he echoed these words of the Lord Jesus, but he did not use His exact words. He prayed, "Lord Jesus, receive my spirit" (Acts 7 : 59). There is a difference. Stephen was being killed, he would die at the hands of his enemies, but he had no power to decide the moment when he would actually die. He was in effect praying that when the moment of death came to him the Lord would receive his spirit. But our Lord was Himself handing over His life and dismissing His spirit into the hands of His Father. It is true that His death was set in motion by men, wicked hands took Him and put Him upon the cross, although even this was within the context of the direct will of God. "Him, being delivered by the determinate counsel and foreknowledge of God, ye have taken, and by wicked hands have crucified and slain" (Acts 2 : 23).

One authority points out that Jesus bowed His head and gave up the ghost, whereas the final act of a dying man is to lift up his head. It is the final act of self-preservation to get as much air as possible into his lungs. Of course after death has taken place his head droops down. But our Lord voluntarily bowed His head and died, as if He were submitting and giving up His life to His Father. The birth of Jesus was supernatural, born of a virgin-mother without a human father, conceived by the Holy Spirit. No one else has ever come into the world in this way, neither has any man lived in the way that Jesus lived. Lord Byron said of Him, "If ever man were God, and God were man, Jesus Christ was both". Nor has any person died as Jesus died, for no one else has decided the moment at which he should die and dismissed his spirit from his body. He was unique in birth, in life and in death.

The wonderful change

It is impossible not to notice that a remarkable change had taken place in the atmosphere on Calvary. The Lord Jesus had been on the cross for six hours. For three of them He suffered the malignity of taunting men, shouting in ridicule at Him, "All that see me laugh me to scorn: they shoot out the lip, they shake the head, saying, He trusted on the Lord that he would deliver him: let him deliver him, seeing he delighted in him" (Psa. 22 : 7-8). "He saved others; himself he cannot save. If he be the king of Israel, let him now come down from the cross, and we will believe him" (Matt. 27 : 42).

Then from twelve until three o'clock the suffering at the hands of men was supplanted by a deeper suffering, suffering at the hands of God. During the hours that the darkness was upon him our Lord entered into the realm of outer darkness and experienced the abandonment and desolation that the penalty of sin incurred, so that He was forsaken even of God. Then the darkness dissolved, the cry of triumph was shouted out, His thirst was quenched and again He is in touch with His Father, "Father into Thy hands I commend my spirit". This is the language of a Son speaking to His Father. Earlier this communion was broken and Jesus cried out "My God, my God . . .". But now their fellowship is re-established with "righteous claims all satisfied". God's countenance is turned again in love upon His Son. It was like the experience of stepping out of deepest darkness into light, like moving from hell to heaven, as indeed it was for the Lord Jesus Christ.

While He was in the hands of men, the Lord suffered great agony of mind, body and spirit. Earlier He had said to His disciples, "The Son of man shall be betrayed into the hands of men: And they shall kill him, and the third day he shall be raised again. And they were exceeding sorry" (Matt. 17 : 22-23). In Gethsemane He came to them, after they had fallen asleep while He was in an agony of prayer, and said to them, "Sleep on now . . . it is enough, the hour is come; behold, the Son of man is betrayed into the hands of sinners. Rise up, let us go; lo, he that betrayeth me is at hand" (Mark 14 : 41). He was in the hands of sinners, and what treatment He received at their hands!

> *"Sinners in derision crowned Him,*
> *Mocking thus the Saviour's claim."*

On the day of Pentecost, Peter charged the people, "Him ye have taken, and by wicked hands have crucified and slain" (Acts 2 : 23). But now came the moment when the hands of men could do no more. He was out of their hands for ever. Never again could He be betrayed by Judas, never again could He be crowned with thorns, never again could He be crucified upon a cross. He was now in the hands of His loving heavenly Father—what different hands, what different treatment He received in these hands. The third day after the crucifixion His Father raised Him from the dead. Crucified in weakness, He was raised by the power of God. Forty days after the resurrection He received Him up into heaven to where He ascended, "far above all principality and power, might and dominion and every name that is named". The mighty hands of the Father conducted His Son in triumph to the highest position of privilege, power and glory at the right hand of His majesty on high. To the Lord Jesus, as the great Mediator, God has given all authority in heaven and on earth. Jesus is on the throne! No longer defeated or in weakness, but reigning with power as Paul tells us, "He must reign till he hath put all his enemies under his feet". The writer to the Hebrews also expresses this thought, "This man, after he had offered one sacrifice for sins for ever, sat down on the right hand of God; From henceforth expecting till his enemies be made his footstool" (chap. 10 : 12-13).

From the Scriptures we learn that one day He will arise from His throne and return to this earth in power and great glory, to be seen by all men, and to usher in His everlasting kingdom which will go on from glory to glory. All this followed upon the act of His committing Himself into His Father's hands.

Communion with God does not depend on time or place

Upon the cross at this point our Lord was in a unique situation. He was still experiencing great suffering; yet He was in close communion with His Father.

So we learn that fellowship with God is not dependent upon time or place, but on a heart relationship with Him. We can be in touch with God, not only in church on Sunday, but at any time and in any place, if our hearts are in the right relationship to Him through the Lord Jesus Christ and under the influence of the Holy Spirit. Daniel, even when in the lions' den, was in wonderful communion with the living God whom he served continually. The three Hebrew boys, when they were thrown into the fiery furnace, were not only untouched by the flames, but were also seen walking freely about with one whom Nebuchadnezzar said was like the Son of God. We shall probably never be thrown into a lions' den or into a furnace of fire, but if fellowship with God is possible there for those who walk closely with Him, surely it is possible in any place. Many saints in our day are called to undergo persecution and endure fiery trials. Their communion with God is often deeper in such experiences than at any other time. Paul and Silas, whilst in prison with their backs bleeding and their feet in stocks, were praising God together in the midst of their suffering.

Jesus said, "Father". Can we say Father when we address God? The Lord could say it because He was uniquely the Son of God. But because of the cross, if we trust in the redemption which Christ bought for us, we can through Him become sons of God. "But as many as received him to them gave he power to become the sons of God, even to them that believe on his name" (John 1 : 12). He died on the cross in order that we too might call God our Father. We can only be sons of God through faith in His Son, but if we have received of God this faith in His son, if we are putting our trust alone in the merits of the blood of Jesus for our eternal salvation then, wherever we are and whenever we come to God, we can, wondrously, call Him Father.

We can experience the security that such a relationship includes of knowing that we are safe as far as our souls are concerned, for time and for eternity. To be, as Jesus was from that moment, in the hands of the Father is to know the greatest security that it is possible for a human being to know, "My Father, which gave them me, is greater than all; and no man is able to pluck them out of my Father's hand" (John 10 : 29).

Better education, the best political party, peace conferences, the United Nations Organisation—though all necessary and helpful in our needy world—can offer us only limited help or hope. But if we are in the Father's hands what need have we to fear? There we are "safe and secure from life's alarms". This is not wishful thinking or a fairy tale philosophy, but eternal glorious fact based upon the revealed Word of God and the Person of His Son Jesus Christ.

"I am the way, the truth, and the life: no man cometh unto the Father, but by me."

"Whosoever believeth in him shall not perish, but shall have everlasting life."